Reaching Resolutions
10 Rules for Success

JOHN A TERRANOVA

Every day we attempt to reach resolutions. In our business, professional, and personal lives; we all try to negotiate our way to resolution. These 10 Rules will focus your efforts and help you successfully reach your resolutions.

Reaching Resolutions
10 Rules for Success

Copyright © 2015
John A Terranova
All rights reserved.
ISBN-13:9781505477979
ISBN 10 1505477972
Library of Congress Control Number: 2015904158
CreateSpace Independent Publishing Platform
North Charleston, South Carolina

In Memory of
John A. Terranova, Sr.

*This book is dedicated
to:
Bernice, my mom;
Miechelle, my bride;
Niki, Sara, Candice, my daughters;
&
Kris, my son.*
Without your love and support,
this book could not have been written.

FOREWORD

Why would anyone want to read, let alone write, a book about negotiating? You know, labor relations, contracts; that stuff.

Ask me 20 years ago and I would not have it said I'd be the one. I knew nothing about negotiating. In fact, when I started in the negotiation "business," I thought my career was ending as it was just starting. It was as if I found myself in a very dark room with no light to help me see what I was facing. I truthfully had no understanding of what I had gotten myself into.

It took some time, but eventually, I began to understand that life – my life, your life - is all about negotiating: *Negotiating to reach a resolution.* We negotiate all the time mostly without realizing it. Whether negotiating a contract for a government agency, a labor union, a private employer or negotiating our way through our lives, the goal is always to reach a resolution. In fact, to me, the term *reaching resolutions* is less intimidating than *negotiating* and it more accurately reflects what we are trying to accomplish.

If you negotiate contracts; then this book can help you. If you don't negotiate contracts but are looking for how to reach resolutions; then this book can help you as well.

Of course, there are other books about how to negotiate. Many of them are either a win at all costs, hate your enemy: stick it to them before they stick it to you interpretation or highly technical treatises on the *science* of negotiating.

Each may be effective in some ways, but they just didn't work for me. Negotiating doesn't have to be that difficult! Once I had discovered that I was really seeking to reach a resolution, then my 10 Rules began to form and fall into place. And when they did, I began to successfully reach my resolutions.

I've negotiated over 50 labor agreements as well as negotiated throughout my life. I had to learn, often the hard way, what worked and what didn't. I want to share my experiences and specifically what worked for me.

Will they work for you? I think they will.

Everything I've written in this book is from my own actual life experiences: my mistakes, and through trial and error, my successes. And it reflects my attempt to simplify the process.

This book began with my career with the State of Illinois, where I spent over a quarter century negotiating contracts, handling employee disputes, training employees, arbitrating and mediating. It continues today with my role as a consultant with The NuLand Group and as the author of the Reaching Resolutions blog. www.reachingresolutionsblog.com

TABLE OF CONTENTS

Part 1: The Background	1
Just Who Am I?	3
My Background	5
Down And Almost Out	7
I'm Not That Smart	9
Part 2: The Preparation	13
I've Got Questions!	15
Negotiate? I Don't Negotiate!	18
I Hate Rules!	20
1st Rule For Reaching Resolutions	23
2nd Rule For Reaching Resolutions	26
3rd Rule For Reaching Resolutions	29
4th Rule For Reaching Resolutions	31
Part 3: The Negotiation	35
5th Rule For Reaching Resolutions	37
6th Rule For Reaching Resolutions (Part 1)	40
You're Part Of The Team, Too! (Part 2)	44
7th Rule For Reaching Resolutions	47
8th Rule For Reaching Resolutions	49
9th Rule For Reaching Resolutions	52
Part 4: Reaching Your Resolution!	55
10th Rule For Reaching Resolutions	57
I Still Can't Get Them To Agree With Me!	59
You Did What??	62
My Mistake	65
How To Deal With Miserable People	68
I'm Mad As Hell! (And I'm Not Going To Take It Anymore!)	72

Be Careful What You Ask For! (Or Another Mistake Made)	75
Mixed Messages	78
Making This Fit	81
From Me To You	83

A successful negotiator doesn't have to be the smartest person in the room, just the person most prepared.

PART 1

THE BACKGROUND

JUST WHO AM I?

This is the part of the book where the author gets to spend your time telling you about all their successes, their triumphs, all the reasons why they're so smart and you should pay attention to him.

Well, I'm not going to do that. Yes, I have spent many years working in the field of negotiations. I've settled employee grievances, argued at arbitration hearings, negotiated numerous contracts, mediated disputes between individuals. I've done all of that.

Blah. Blah. Blah. Truth is, I'm a lot like you. I struggle too. In my attempts to reach resolutions, things weren't all that easy.

No matter where you are, what you do – Life is a struggle. We all are ultimately forced to learn how to either coexist or fail. Someone smarter than me probably once said "Life is a series of transactions." I don't actually know if someone did say that, but if you think about it, seems to be true.

We interact by transacting. Exchanging money, ideas, work, we give to get. Or maybe even, we give something in order to keep our status quo. However you look at it: it's a transaction. And we negotiate each transaction.

Of all my aspirations in life, I've discovered that being happy ranks at or near the top. And, I've found that whenever I've reached that state of happiness it's also when I've reached a resolution. A resolution to: a problem; a question; a contract; employee dispute; or really any type of life transaction.

As I said, it took me awhile to figure this out. When I began, I felt as if I was in a dark room. I couldn't see my way ahead. Gradually though, bit by bit, I began to feel my way around the "room" and eventually begin to "see" the light.

While I do believe this book will help those who negotiate for a living; I also think this will help those of you who aren't professional negotiators – people who negotiate in life trying to reach resolutions.

In fact, the same guiding principles I used in negotiating contracts I also try to use in my daily life. It was all trial and error, mistake after mistake, before that light turned on. I actually reviewed what happened and why, what worked and didn't work.

I discovered that there were steps or Rules that, when I followed them, I had success. And when I didn't follow them, I didn't have success. What was my definition of success? You guessed it! Success occurred when I had reached a resolution. And resolution pointed me in the direction of being happy!

These rules led to this book. I don't think of this as a "self-help" book, rather, it's my observations on how I was able to reach resolutions in my life – professional as well as personal. They actually "de-mystified" negotiating contracts and my reaching resolutions for me. These rules worked for me and if you try them out, I think they'll work for you as well.

MY BACKGROUND

How does one begin a career in Labor Relations? Do you have to get a specific degree? Do you have to be a lawyer? I didn't, and I'm not, so for me, the answer was easy: no.

I certainly didn't set out to be negotiator. To be honest, I really wanted to go into politics. I graduated from college with a degree in Economics. My motivation to get that degree was simply because I thought it would help my credentials in seeking public office. In other words, "Oh, this guy must be smart; he's got a freaking degree in Economics!"

As I was nearing graduation I went to see my counselor who asked me what I intended to do with my Economics degree. Trust me, there weren't many job openings calling for an Econ degree. I told him about my desire to go into politics. I even confessed that I was unsure if the degree would be enough. I think I was getting cold feet about actually moving into the real world outside of school. So my counselor advised me to either go to law school or pursue a Master's degree in Public Administration.

I thought about it. Being a lawyer would be cool. But I was impatient and probably a bit lazy, too. Law school would mean 3 more years vs. the MA taking 2 more years. And if I attended class in the summer I could get the MA in 18 months! I was already approaching my mid-twenties (!) so I chose getting my Masters. And in a short year and a half, I got a Master's degree in Public Administration. Now, also understand that although I thought it would be cool to be a lawyer, I didn't really want to practice law. Like the Economics major, I thought a law degree sure would look good on my resume! But in my impatience, I didn't want to spend any more time in school than I had to.

So a Master's degree! Surely that had to train me in labor relations! Well…, no not really. I took one course in Collective Bargaining. That was it. Now certainly there are college courses, degrees, etc. in Labor Relations. I just don't think you need to do that if you want to negotiate: whether it be contracts or your life.

Prior to leaving graduate school, I had always worked in the customer service arena in some way, shape or form. I worked in a grocery store's produce section, in a department store, the circulation department of our local newspaper, even delivered newspapers and worked as a meat cutter.

In fact, working as a meat cutter allowed me to work for my Dad and also, for a time, with my brother.

My Dad adjusted my schedule so I could both work and go to school full time. For 6 years, I was able to work side by side with him, getting to see him in a different light. Not just as a parent, but also as a supervisor and how he treated others – employees, customers, salesmen.

Definitely saw a different side of him. And I discovered how others saw my dad, too.

Life was all good. Until I got laid off…

DOWN AND ALMOST OUT

Out of work! I got laid off from my job as a meat cutter! I had just graduated with my Master's degree the month before! Supporting a family, now what do I do? And to add to my drama, I had just announced I would be running for political office – a seat on our County Board. Who would vote for an unemployed meat cutter with a Master's degree?

I applied for every job opening I could find. I went on a few interviews but nothing happened. And then, I fell into the job with the Illinois (IL) Department of Corrections. But it wasn't a straight drop into the job; it was more of a roundabout, circular, bumpy fall.

My political mentor, the person I was running to replace was retiring, and she told me that unless I hired a campaign manager to manage my campaign, she would run again. What? I was running for a part time office! I didn't know anyone who would be my manager. I ended up calling the local party chairman who gave me a name or two and suggested I also contact my State Representative to get his take.

I called the State Rep, leaving a message, then called the first name on my list of two, and told her my tale of woe. This was someone I had never met; a real cold call if there was one. And she explained she was several months pregnant and would be very limited in what she could do. I didn't hear much other that "…what she could do." You're hired!

She cautioned me to slow down and also suggested I continue asking around. By then, the State Rep returned my call and I told him my dilemma. No job, just graduated, running for the county board and needing to hire a manager. He said two things to me: My choice for a campaign manager was a good one, even expecting a child and limited in her involvement he thought she would be excellent; and he asked if I liked to work with kids. Why yes! Yes I do!

Turns out, my degrees were in the social science field which was a qualification for working in the State's Department of Corrections - Juvenile Parole Division. I interviewed, trying not to sound too desperate and just like that, after being an unemployed political candidate for a few months, I was going to be working in the public sector.

I now was a Juvenile Parole Agent. No negotiation needed. Unless convincing young teenagers to stay on the straight and narrow without getting into trouble again demanded certain negotiation skills. Some of my co-workers viewed the job as simply maintaining order while others believed in changing the kids' outlooks: on themselves, their families, and their communities. These employees sincerely tried to make a difference in the kid's lives. It was a great experience, but still very little negotiating skills needed.

I'M NOT THAT SMART

So here I was a Parole Agent working with the Illinois Department of Corrections! A State Employee! It wasn't long though, a mere 5 years, before I applied to transfer to a new State run program called the Upward Mobility Program (UMP). The position would be a promotion for me. The UMP program, negotiated by the State and one of its employee unions, would encourage training and educational opportunities for employees to use for career advancement. It was run by the University of Illinois and as an employee, I would be able to take University courses at a highly reduced rate! Plus I was getting a pay raise! Sign me up!

But, as fate would have it, two weeks before I was to begin the job, I received a call from the Director of another state agency, the Department of Central Management Services (CMS), informing me that I would instead become his employee as the Upward Mobility Program was now under his agency. Not the University of Illinois. No opportunity for free tuition. Instead, the program would be under the labor relations division of CMS.

I didn't choose the labor relations field. Someone in a state bureaucracy decided to move a program from one end of the government to another. And that was it.

I'm now in labor relations where I would be handling employee grievances. I'd be settling their disputes. I would also begin negotiating labor contracts. I would be working to reach an agreement that would determine how much an employee would be paid, what benefits they would enjoy, even what their working conditions would be like. And I knew nothing about this field!

But before I could delve further into this new career, I had to do something. I had to get trained!

My first assignment was to attend a two day training seminar on the State of Illinois' primary collective bargaining agreement. I was told I needed to be trained on the union contract that covered the UMP program.

OK, I'm ready for this, or so I thought. Traveling to Chicago, I went to the State's J.R Thompson Center and entered a large class room. After an hour, listening to the first few articles of the contract, I was completely bored out of my mind. The subject was so dry I had difficulty staying awake. It was painful.

And so, I did what seemed to make the most sense to me at the time: I took a really long lunch. I came back about an hour after the afternoon session began. The next day I came in late in the morning and then took another long lunch.

"What had I got myself into?" I remembered thinking. I should have stayed with working with juvenile delinquents. It was easier.

Oh, and by the way, the instructor of that boring training turned out to be one of my new supervisors. My labor relations career was off to a roaring start. After this auspicious beginning, would I ever learn what I was doing? Somehow, I had to hang in there and try to learn about this career I "chose."

In time, I got to meet Karma. You know karma too, I bet. Either I had a penchant for talking or I was being punished for skipping out on those sessions, because within the next year I was "promoted" to teach that very same training seminar! Twice a month, every month.

Now what do I do? I mean, I could barely stay awake attending the training, how was I going to teach it?

With no choice in the matter, I did what I had to do. I had to make the subject matter more interesting *to me*. I did what I had been doing most of my life: I told stories. And, I tried to make the training personal to the audience. I ended up doing that training for over 20 years. My formula stayed the same – tell stories and make it enjoyable.

And that's what I've attempted to do here.

PART 2

THE PREPARATION

I'VE GOT QUESTIONS!

At every training seminar I teach, I usually start off the session by asking the audience to describe "successful negotiations." I typically get a variety of answers but eventually the "right" answer comes out: successful negotiations are the ones where both sides are satisfied with the outcome. That's to say: when both sides got something they wanted.

I also get asked similar questions on reaching resolutions so I thought I'd share some of them here.

Here's a sample of what I typically get asked:

1. Are you really that smart? Or variations like "You must be very smart, aren't you?"

OK, I really don't get that a lot. But I always prepare this answer just in case. Uh, well...Yes I am!

Truth is, I'm no smarter than anyone else. To be successful in negotiating or reaching resolutions, you need common sense and the ability to know what you want and what you're prepared to give up.

2. Is negotiating difficult?

No, not really. I look at negotiations as simply a process used to reach a resolution. Sometimes we intimidate ourselves by thinking that only experts can negotiate. Sometimes things are only as difficult as we make them out to be.

3. Do I need a lawyer to negotiate on my behalf?

I think this myth is perpetuated by attorneys. It's simply not true. Successful resolutions are most often realized by using simple common sense on both sides. Lawyers are trained to be litigants, they argue points of law. That is not negotiating!

4. Will college prepare me for negotiating?

Any courses on collective bargaining may help but certainly it's not necessary. I had one course on collective bargaining and it taught me the history of collective bargaining, not how to negotiate.

5. Have you ever made a mistake?

A mistake? No, several. I continually have had to learn and then relearn how to reach resolutions. I've shared more than a few in this book. And as a bonus, when you do make mistakes, you can write about them in a blog or even a book.

6. If I make a mistake, won't everyone laugh and then not respect me?

First, everyone makes mistakes. Second, the key is how you respond to your mistake. And take it from me, if you can laugh at yourself, you won't notice the others laughing with you.

7. Have you ever had to deal with someone you just don't like?

Yes I have, on several occasions. Life sometimes involves dealing with miserable, crappy people. I've discovered there are 2 ways to deal with them. Change my reaction; or avoid them.

8. What if I'm a shy person and have difficulty speaking aloud?

Well, at some point you'll have to speak out to get what you want. If you don't, how will anyone know what it is you want? The point is that negotiating isn't about who yells the loudest. There are people who do negotiate like that. Usually they lose.

9. What if I don't know what to do?

Well, to be self-serving; you should continue reading this book or read the blog.
And I must say that I've always felt that in order to reach a resolution, you have to prepare. You have to become an "expert" in the field/issue you are negotiating or at the very least surround yourself with experts. That's what I usually do. I surround myself with people smarter than me.

10. Am I too old to reach my resolutions?

You are never too old. Every day we are "transacting" with each other. We only stop reaching resolutions when we stop trying.

11. Does reaching a resolution always make you happy?

For me it does. Why? Because I believe that everyday life contains a series of "transactions." We give and take in everyday life. My goal in life is to be happy. If I can reach a resolution, then yes I'm happy!

NEGOTIATE? I DON'T NEGOTIATE!

As I've mentioned, I've spent a long time - over a quarter century – as a professional negotiator. But, what about you? Do you negotiate in your life? Do you think you even negotiate at all?   No?

Well not to be disagreeable, but I think maybe you do.

Again, the premise of this book is this: we all negotiate at some level: at work; at home; in our everyday lives. And ultimately, we negotiate to reach some resolution.

Why are we doing this?   Is it the hope we'll take everything from someone else or just getting our fair share?

Think about it. We do it so often we don't call it negotiating.   Maybe arguing is probably more like it.   Or "conning" someone out of something! We want that raise, that promotion. We want our price on that car in the showroom. We want...a lot. Sometimes we want so many things we can't figure out what we want first! And to be honest, I've done my share of arguing too.

I know *why* I've been negotiating all these years, I got paid. Yet I regularly "negotiate" or "bargain" over things in my personal life too.

There's a guy I know. He fancies himself a negotiator, a true businessman. "We need to run (fill in the blank) like a business!" But his "negotiating" skills are simply to out-talk, often and louder, then the other guy.

That's it! That's his strategy. And sometimes he gets his way. Why? Because most people won't deal with him and those that do just want him to stop yelling. That's not negotiating - that's bullying.

Here is what I think of when it comes to negotiating. It took me awhile to realize that:

Negotiating (anything) is simply knowing what you want and what you are willing to do (or give) to get it; to reach a resolution.

Am I willing to give up X and Y in order to get, what I really want, Z? Is giving up X too expensive a price to pay for Z? If you're going to be successful, you learn quickly to prioritize!

In my mind, successful negotiating is not about taking everything from others. Sometimes we have to give things up too. It's all about reaching resolutions.

I HATE RULES!

I don't know about you but I never really liked rules. I actually hated them. I remember, as a young boy, my mom told me it was important to follow rules, (Did all parents do this?) and so I told her that rules were for other people because I was the exception. And, every Rule has one.

Even then I thought I had an answer for everything. Thought I was being clever. Don't know exactly what Mom thought but pretty sure "he's so clever" wasn't it. (Pretty sure she still loved me anyway.)

But, I really don't like rules and I'm betting you don't either. Rules were always for the other guys not me.

I learned at an early age if I really needed something I could go all out and just take care of it. If a term paper needed to be done, I did it the night before it was due. Sleep was optional, not mandatory. Homework could always be done in the class before I needed to hand it in. I did enough to get by. The 'rules' about proper preparation didn't apply.

At work it was the same, I could get assignments done last-minute. No one was the wiser, and the boss loved my work. It was easy. Friends needed something - no sweat - I got it done, maybe not always on time. I was super busy! But they could all count on me. Yet...something was missing. I wasn't accomplishing all that I thought I should. Every time I thought I had everything figured out, something would happen. Something unexpected or something I forgot to do. OK, maybe I didn't plan things out very well, I didn't always have to. Things worked out before, why not now?

It was as if I was working/living to put out fires and not really succeeding to a level of actual achievement.

Now if you're thinking I had one of those "A Ha" moments, I didn't. I would think about it and vow to change only to fall back taking things easy. I'd figure it out - I needed to be better organized, or maybe get more serious about whatever it was, or get more disciplined.

Maybe I'd read more books on the subject before I tackled the problem. Maybe I would just procrastinate and do everything at the last-minute. I was often at my best "flying by the seat of my pants." I read that sometimes our problems in life were the result of not saying "no" enough. I took that to mean say "No" to everything.

Or maybe the solution was to say "Yes" to everything, I forget. So I went through a "Yes" to everything period too.

In my martial arts training, I learned that to be a master of anything, one must be able to focus on the smallest detail and perform it well. The mere task of preparing tea, pouring and serving it could mark one as a "Master". In Eastern thought, if one is a Master at one thing it also meant that they were a Master in other areas, one to be respected and, in some cases, feared. There is the story of a fierce samurai warrior coming to a village to challenge a local samurai. He stopped by the dwelling of the local samurai to share tea. Upon observing the detail and precision of the local master in serving tea, he knew this was not a warrior to challenge. After drinking his tea, the Samurai thanked his host and then slipped out of the village.

The message I took from this story was to be very good at details. OK, but how could I master the details? I had always thought of myself as a big picture guy. How then could I be a Master of details?

Would it lead to me being a "Master of Negotiating?" Maybe I didn't have the patience or the focus needed to succeed.

Eventually I discovered that, for me to be successful, I needed some help. If there were structures (procedures, guidelines) I could follow along in the little things of my life, maybe the bigger things in life would become easier to achieve.

So...I...made...a...decision...to Follow some rules!

I know, I know I said it before: I really don't like Rules. But, something had to change.

This book is about rules for Reaching Resolutions. These 10 Rules, through trial and error, came to life, over time. There were many steps forward only to fall back and being forced to start over again.

These rules worked first in my career, negotiating contracts, and then in my approach to life's curves, valleys and peaks.

These 10 Rules for Success actually helped me focus on what I needed to do to reach resolutions. They also helped simplify my efforts to reach a resolution.

Now, if you're thinking this book will teach you how to get everything you ever wanted by "negotiating" for yourself without regard for the other person - you'll be disappointed. I've never been a fan of the take it or leave it persuasion. I also think that attempting to make every situation a "win-win" isn't always attainable either. Sometimes it comes down to simply "what can you live with?"

I recently met with a client, who I have known for over 15 years, to negotiate a contract. She gave me a list of what her group wanted to get. Before I could respond, she said to me, "I know you are going to ask me what I'm prepared to give up in order to get what we want." She was right. It doesn't always have to work out to be a "win-win" situation, but no one gives up anything for nothing.

OK, I convinced myself! I need rules!

1ST RULE FOR REACHING RESOLUTIONS

Do you remember the movie *"Fight Club?"* Remember the Rules?

- "The first rule of Fight Club is: You do not talk about Fight Club.
- The second rule of Fight Club is: You do not talk about Fight Club.
- Third rule of Fight Club: Someone yells stop, goes limp, taps out, the fight is over.
- Fourth rule: Only two guys to a fight.
- Fifth rule: One fight at a time, fellas.
- Sixth rule: No shirts, no shoes.
- Seventh rule: Fights will go on as long as they have to.
- And the eighth and final rule: If this is your first night at Fight Club, you have to fight." *Fight Club; 1996 "Tyler Durden" (Edward Norton/Brad Pitt) David Fincher (Director)*

In life, just like the movie, there are always going to be rules, or guidelines, or laws, or orders. Rules that one would need to follow in order to get anything done successfully.

Over time, as my labor relations career developed, I discovered this list of Rules to follow whenever I negotiated contracts, and then in dealing with my life situations, trying to reach my resolutions.

So here we go:

10 Rules for Reaching Resolutions
1st Rule

Whenever, I'm negotiating or settling disputes, or trying to make sense of why people are how they are (rude, mean, unfriendly) I have to remember **RULE #1. Don't take it personally.**

Every training seminar I've held – this Number One Rule is always announced right off the top. "Don't take it personally." Even if the other person who's making life difficult for you IS making it personal, ***don't take it personally.***

I once sat across a union representative at the negotiation table who would practice venting his spleen on whatever unfortunate person sat on the other side. That day, it was me. Now, I don't know what function the spleen has, I just know I caught the vent. And when he let loose, I did what I sometimes do when I'm nervous or feeling unsure - I started to smile and then to laugh. Not laughing loudly, just a laugh response that prompted Spleen Venter to stop his tirade to demand to know why I was laughing. I told him I had never met anyone who could string so many profanities together and still make sense! His sentences were all adjectives! He started to smile and then to laugh. And then, and only then, were we able to get to the business at hand.

Later on, he told me that his cursing technique didn't work as well on me, because it was hard to yell at someone who wasn't fazed by it. Most people were either deeply offended by him or felt they had to respond in kind, thereby escalating the argument. Not much would get accomplished and no one wanted to deal with him. And he apparently liked it that way. His strategy or, rather his negotiating technique, was to make everything personal.

Supervisors would often ask me how to deal with employee grievances or complaints. After questioning them on the situation, I discovered what really aggravated the supervisor was how in the world the employee could complain about them or their work! "I'm right and they're wrong!" It often wasn't the actual issue that upset the supervisor. They were upset because they were taking the complaint personally.

As I negotiated contracts and heard grievances one thing always held true: the moment I took the situation personally, I lost focus on what should have been the most important aspect - my end goal. I had to get over taking it personally before I could re-focus and move forward.

Now before you comment that this is too simplistic and not very realistic let me pose this - look back on situations when you lost it - no matter the situation - when you lost it, who then had control of the situation? It doesn't matter how insulting the other person was or if you were in the right. The moment you take it personally, you lose the ability to deal with the situation in a fair, impartial and objective way. I know this is easier said than done, no one wants to be insulted, cursed or yelled at. But ultimately your level of success will be determined by your ability to adhere to this Rule.

I still struggle with this sometimes, but when I look back on the failed negotiation sessions, the failed meetings where nothing is accomplished, often I find the reason was simply failing to adhere to Rule #1.

Rule #1: Don't take it personally!

2ND RULE FOR REACHING RESOLUTIONS

Rule #1 was **Don't Take it Personally!**

You might be thinking that's real easy for me. I've done this for almost 30 years. Nothing fazes me.

Well it's true. Nothing fazes me... until it does. Ask my wife, or my kids, or for that matter, anyone who knows me.

Even when I'm on my game, it sometimes is STILL a real struggle. We all have feelings, right? When I'm working on a contract I know not to take anything personally. I'm getting paid to not take it personal. Yet sometimes I still do.

I didn't want to feel that I wasn't good enough to sit at the table. If they yelled at me, I wanted to yell back. If I was criticized, I sometimes felt I had to defend myself.

Needless to say, whenever this happened, I "felt" good about myself because I stood up and defended myself. In reality, the reality of reaching a resolution, I hadn't accomplished anything at all at the negotiating table. I mistakenly believed I had to respond to everything to make sure the other side knew I deserved to be there.

And so the process would just drag on. In those early negotiating days, the sessions would take forever to finish.

REACHING RESOLUTIONS 27

As soon as I figured out that the other person deliberately tried to get me to react personally so they could take control of the session, I have to admit it become somewhat easier for me. I was such a quick study; it only took me a few years to fully realize it.

"But that's at work," you say! "Not everything at work applies to my life! Certainly Not My Personal Life!"

Well, let's look at that, too. I knew another guy. You probably do too. This guy was the most miserable, unhappy person I think I'd ever met. Even when he was happy, he wasn't! Nothing was his fault. He took ownership of nothing - his life, his job, his friends (both of them), or the truth.

I had known this guy awhile but didn't really have any close dealings with him so I simply had thought everything was cool between us. Apparently, it wasn't. He started out saying things behind my back. After a while, I became aware of it and went to him - surely it can't be true. He told me I was mistaken. He would never do that. I let it go.

As you can guess, he continued his chirping and I kept hearing about it. I went to him again, this time angry. I still can't believe he's doing this, right? He gave me no satisfaction, said "it's all in the past, forget about it." What? So, he did actually say all that "stuff?" He had lied to me! I can't believe it! Now I'm upset and angry.

"Why did this happen to me?" I spent a month of my life trying to figure out just what was going on. I took it personally. The stories he made up - after I came to my senses - were ridiculous! If any of my real friends believed any of it, well they couldn't be that smart after all - That's how utterly ridiculous they were. To this day I can't believe I let it bother me. FOR--A--MONTH!!

Once I saw what was really happening, an extremely bitter, unhappy person who, for whatever reason, decided I was the cause for his own miserable state of life, I was able to distance my personal feelings away from this mess. Then, I could decide to deal or not deal with his issues.

This happened to me even though at that time I had spent some years as a professional negotiator. I had the skill to know not to take things personally but I still did. I couldn't understand why someone I didn't really have much interaction with could be so spiteful, vindictive, so unhappy.... and then take it out on me!

I wasn't joking when I said earlier - Nothing Fazes Me - until it does.

So there you have it. This rule applies to any situation you may encounter. It is such an important Rule to remember that I do repeat it at every seminar I've ever given be it: negotiating; handling employee complaints; or in life.

So for a quick review: If Rule #1 is **Don't take it Personally** Then it stands to follow that the 2nd rule has to be:

RULE #2: DON'T TAKE IT PERSONALLY! I really mean it!

3ʳᴰ RULE FOR REACHING RESOLUTIONS

Have you ever been talking to a friend where both of you are speaking yet not connecting? I don't mean where you are miles apart and will probably never reach agreement. No, I mean when you both are making the exact same point but your friend is disagreeing and then attempts to convince you to agree to his point which is the same point you just made. The conversations usually go back and forth where one of you, (in my life, it's always the other person) keeps saying "I know but…" and then re-explains the same thing you just said. I understand my point, why can't they stop and listen to me? Frustrating right? You both are saying the exact same thing but no one is in agreement. The discussion (argument) just keeps going.

Well, that brings us to Rule #3 - **Know the language**.

We're talking communication here. In life and in negotiations, the ability to communicate is essential. Now I do assume that everyone we regularly communicate with speaks a similar language. But, if you can't speak the same language on roughly the same level you might just as well forget reaching a resolution.

I don't mean to imply the intellectual level has to be equal, just that you need to know where they're coming from and if possible, where they want to end up.

I once negotiated a contract for a large State agency and the other side's negotiator spent the entire morning session explaining and re-explaining a very technical, detailed point about his side's proposal. Not being technically astute, I had no idea what he was proposing, what he wanted, or even what he said. That session at the table went nowhere. After we broke into our respective caucus groups, I pulled him aside and told him my problem with his proposal. I had no idea what he was talking about! He told me he had prepared his presentation extensively, knowing it was important to his side. I think he also wanted to impress his team with his vast knowledge of what they did at work. Not a bad strategy to use with his team, but it didn't help me to understand it, especially if he wanted me to agree to it! After some discussion I finally understood. Turned out what he wanted really wasn't a big deal to my side, he just didn't know how else to propose it.

This is a cliché, I know, but communication is *always the key* and not just in speaking but listening as well. Sometimes we're faced with a person who always needs to talk, sometimes over you. They talk and talk because they don't want to hear what you have to say. You won't get far. I tend to avoid those people. If I can't, then I have to focus hard so that when they do come up for air I can make my point in the conversation. Just as it's important I understand what they are trying to say, they also have to understand my point before any resolution is possible.

Sometimes we have to dig a bit to discover what the other person is saying in order to reach a resolution.

Sometimes all we need do is listen....

Rule #3 Know the Language

4TH RULE FOR REACHING RESOLUTIONS

When I was younger I remember my Dad talking about Franklin Delano Roosevelt. He was a young boy when FDR was first elected President. Dad told me that during the run up to World War II, FDR was giving a speech somewhere denouncing war and said, "I hate war! Eleanor (his wife) hates war! And...(Dramatic pause) I hate Eleanor!"

We would laugh at this, "I hate Eleanor!" How funny. I never knew if FDR really said that. It didn't matter, my Dad said he did. He was pretty young when FDR was President so I don't know if he got the quote right or wrong. Or maybe it was one of those times when he and his friends would make things up and over his life time it became his truth. It didn't matter to me. But it was one of those moments I've always remembered. Dad laughed, I laughed. All was right in the world.

I can still picture in my mind the image of FDR, his cigarette holder pointed up and through clenched teeth, growling "And I hate Eleanor!"

As I got older I often retold that story. I'd get some laughs, sometimes quizzical looks. "Really FDR said that?" "Yes!" I'd say, "My Dad told me so." But, over time something happened. I began to wonder why FDR would say such a thing about his wife. Can you imagine the outrage if President Obama said something like that about his wife, Michelle!

Yet for so many years it was real to me. Why? *Because it was my Dad telling me*! When I was a boy (and I don't think I ever outgrew it) my Dad was big, strong, and funny, a real scorch! Sometimes his bark was loud but then he'd flash his compassionate side. He taught us right from wrong. I never knew him to actually get into a fist fight, (though there were some close encounters!) but we all knew he could back up his words! I wanted to be just like him. I think all of us kids did.

I know this isn't unique just to me. We all have someone or something that we place all our faith, our trust, maybe even our lives on the line for: a belief or cause or person. It's not wrong. We all do it. Sometimes we are told from birth just what to believe, what is real. It's not necessarily wrong, but we need to learn to recognize it when it happens.

Why? As we negotiate contracts or life, we need to be open to the fact that sometimes our beliefs, thoughts or actions aren't always based on what's real or true. We need to discover what IS real or true for us - before we can experience success. You can't successfully negotiate anything if you're operating under a false belief. Your foundation (argument) will crumble.

So does this mean my Dad was wrong? Was his story not real?

I guess I could Google the story to be certain but it doesn't matter anymore. My Dad may have been right or wrong - MY reality is the moment he and I shared laughing at his story. That's what is real to me.

If reality isn't always what we perceive, then we must find what is real and true. Often times, what is real for me is not real for you. I see the sky as blue, you see it as black. We each have a perception of what is real - seen through our own unique lenses. Each of us thinks we are right. So what's the solution?

We need to be more open, and not more closed, minded. In negotiations, after you discover your reality, you need to discover the other side's reality, where they are coming from and, if possible, why.

The goal here is to *be aware*, to *be awake* to what is *actually happening*, in our lives. Real life often isn't good or bad - it just is. And it often doesn't wait for us wake up and take notice. And if we don't notice it- what's real and true just might smack us in the face. We won't see it coming and then watch out!

Which brings us to:

RULE #4 Know What's Real.

PART 3

THE NEGOTIATION

5TH RULE FOR REACHING RESOLUTIONS

Here's an easy question. What is it that you want?

At times it's not so easy to answer. There's so much to choose! Maybe I want this one. Or that one! I can't decide!! The truth of the matter is that many times we don't know what we want.

And so, Rule #5 is **Know What You Want!** You'll never be a successful negotiator - in any forum - unless you know what it is that you're seeking!

A few years ago, I represented an employer at the negotiating table and I asked them the question: What do you want? It led to the following:

> ME: "What is it that you want?" THEM: "Nothing."
> ME: "Really, there's nothing you want?" THEM: "No not really."
> ME: "Seriously?" THEM: "Yes, let's just keep the status quo."
> Finally, they had told me something! They wanted no changes!

So, I proceeded to negotiate under that mandate, no changes to the contract. Until, near the end of our negotiations, my client decided they *did* want something....they wanted to impose an *Employee Appearance Dress Code* on their employees! Something NO OTHER group of employees had in their contract! If you're wondering, this proposed change would determine: how long your hair could be (male and female); how long or short your facial hair, (sideburns, beards, mustaches) whether you could wear jewelry, (male or female) or how much facial make up, etc. These employees were already required to wear uniforms, now we wanted to regulate how each employee groomed themselves!

I'm not saying this was a bad or a good thing. I was fairly certain that someone back at their office had panicked and thought we had better be getting something big in this negotiation! However, we ultimately made our position weaker because by asking for our "had to have" proposal late in the game; the union knew one thing was now certain.

If we were to have any chance of getting what we now wanted, then we were going to have to pay for it. And we did. We ended up getting the new dress code but it cost us! Literally, it cost us. Big. We ended up giving bonus payments! How did this happen to us?

We weren't smart about *what* we wanted and *when* we wanted to ask for it. We waited so long to make up our mind on what we really wanted, we made it more difficult for ourselves to get it. The other side knew how important it was to us so they determined we would have to give up plenty for it. We might not have had to pay as much if we would have started out knowing what we really wanted.

Bottom line for this employer: They were extremely happy to get the new grooming code but they were very unhappy about how much they had to pay for it. Not quite the victory it could have been.

In life situations, we all think we know just what it is that we want. But do we really? I should know better, but I have started the day prepared to do one thing only to change course and go in a complete opposite way. This sounded good but so does this!

I've started so many things only to get interested in something else before I finished what I had originally started. And when I do this I end up NOT accomplishing anything! I never reach a resolution!

You've heard the saying; "Life can throw us curves," right? Why throw curves at ourselves as well?

So how do I know what I want?   When I meet with clients I always ask them:

- What is it exactly that you want?
- What change would you like to see?
- What's broken and needs to be fixed?
- What costs/expenses needs to be addressed?
- What do you need to operate more efficiently?

And since this works with them, in my life I ask myself these very same questions.

Getting the answers enables us to then plan our strategies: How to get from "A" to "B" in order to achieve "C".

It's what works for me to get what I want to reach my particular resolution.

You would think this should be an easy question to answer. I have found, however, oftentimes it's not.

Think about it.....

Rule #5 Know What You Want.

6TH RULE FOR REACHING RESOLUTIONS (PART 1)

When you negotiate in life, do you have a team? Or do you fly solo?

Remember when we were kids and would pick sides for some game? I always wanted to be a captain so I could pick my team. Why? To make sure I didn't get picked last. No one wants to be the last pick.

I never wanted to hurt anyone's feelings either so my last pick was always the youngest kid. I kind of felt sorry for them, always wanting to play with us big kids.

Well, in negotiating contracts ....FORGET about picking your own team. It doesn't happen. Oh sure, maybe occasionally you get to pick some members to assist you, but picking your team? No, someone else usually makes that call.

But that's OK. Really it is.

I've always believed only one person per side actually negotiates. You know: One speaker. One representative. Now that doesn't mean you act all alone either. You have a team, with you, supporting you, helping you.

In my negotiating life, I've had all sorts of personalities on my teams. There were "Loud" to "Quiet" types. And "Hardworking" to "Hardly showing up for the sessions" types, too.

During my entire career I never picked my team. Not once. Since I represented various employers, they always decided who would be sent to assist me. And after a few sessions it was always clear who would go the extra mile, stay late, be engaged in the process and who would not. The strong team members quickly separated themselves from the others.

I should also mention that I never refused any management personnel from joining our team. I always felt if they or their employer had a stake in the outcome of the process, then they could join in. It was also not uncommon that my side outnumbered the union's team.

As I've written above, I've had all sorts of personalities on my teams. But couldn't the large number of members prove unruly or at best difficult to lead? No, not really.

So how did I deal with them? Well, just like the "rules for reaching resolutions" we also have a set of rules for our team too!

With respect to the number of employers I've worked with and for, I have adapted some of their long-standing guides for my use.

Here they are:

Rules for My Team

1. There is only one spokesperson at the table - And it's me!

Translation - Once we are meeting with the other side YOU DON"T SAY ANYTHING unless called upon... by me! This avoids the other side's attempt to split our team and insures we speak with a united voice.

2. When at the table, assume a POKER face.

Translation- No expressions, no head shaking, no emotional flashes whatsoever!

3. As your employer's representative you are responsible for keeping your principals notified of every development.

4. If your employer wants specific proposals to be advocated, it's your job to explain the proposals to other members of the team and if requested, provide background information as well.

5. When in our caucus or team meetings, you have every right to speak up and voice your opinions. I will do everything I can to advance your proposal. However once we reach a point in the process where we won't progress further, I retain the veto power to withdraw your proposal for the common good.

6. If we work late into the evening, you are expected to do likewise. If you are not in attendance when decisions are made, well... too bad for you (and your employer)!

7. In addition to number 6, don't tell your employer you are at negotiations when you're really taking time off. Whatever your reason is, the team and I won't cover for you.

8. If the other side presents a proposal and information on the possible impacts to your employer is needed, you are responsible to collect that info. For example, if you're asked how many employees work a particular shift – don't guess! Get the correct headcount.

9. Treat all discussions - both at the negotiating table and in our caucus meetings - in the strictest confidence!

Translation – DO NOT repeat what's been said!

10. Lastly, as in Life, DON'T Take Things Personally! Oftentimes, things are said at the table to provoke a reaction: DO NOT BECOME THE REACTION!

Think these are pretty simplistic? Well, I've experienced violations on every one of these rules over the years. I've had team members speak at the table, members not show up for sessions, even had one go to the union and suggest proposals that "we would agree to." AND this was done behind my back too!

To minimize the likelihood of that happening, at the beginning of every negotiation, I meet with the team and go over these rules. I tell them I will do everything I can to advance their agendas - proposals, positions etc. I even go over my style of negotiating.

Now, in my negotiating style, I tend to be less formal, asking questions to get the other side on the record as they respond, I don't usually get upset unless I need to make a point. Sometimes I may even crack wise. The key is that I want to remain in control while slowly lessening the other side's ability to control the sessions.

One time I had just gone over these rules in my team's caucus meeting. We went to the table and the union began presenting their proposals to us. I asked a simple question to the union, wanting them to further explain what it was they were seeking on one of their demands. And, I wanted to get their response recorded in our notes.

Suddenly, to my immediate right, one of my team members, a co-worker, decided to speak up and explain the union's position to me! She was surprised I didn't understand the other side's position! The union didn't even attempt to explain - my side did it for them!

Oh, I had some fun with her when we got back to our caucus room!

In spite of the above example, these Team Rules really have been successful for me. The team benefits by knowing what's expected of them too.

Give them a try to see if they don't also work for you.

Who's on YOUR side?

YOU'RE PART OF THE TEAM, TOO!
(PART 2)

The first section focused on your team and their responsibilities. But what about you, you're part of the team too. What should you be like? That's why there's a Part Two.

Although many negotiators trying to reach resolutions are domineering, dictatorial, wait I'm searching for another "d" word... I've found the path to successful negotiating to resolution is best accomplished by service - to your employer, your team and to yourself.

I once worked for, not directly under thankfully, an individual so wrapped up in his notion of power that he was an absolute hindrance to accomplishing anything. He didn't attempt to inspire. He intended to intimidate.

A few years back I was wrapping up a contract. We were ready to settle and I jumped through every hoop he created. All that was left was a simple telephone conference to go over the details of the settlement. Details he had insisted upon. I cleared everything with his assistant right down to submitting all my talking points for his approval days prior to the call. Everything he asked for, I delivered. I triple checked my proposal and informed the union that I would need a conference room and telephone to get final approval from my principal. And then at the time I was directed to call him, I did just that.

I got his assistant on the line, who patched me into his highness' office. He asked who I was. I identified myself and explained my call succinctly. I was then asked where my supervisor was and I answered he was negotiating another contract. I again stated the reason for my call - per his request, I was calling to finalize the settlement terms of this contract, where I was located, even reminding him that we had previously met in his office. He then asked where our staff attorney was - I was dumbfounded but answered honestly - "He's in Greece on vacation."

And with that response, there was a screech as if the telephone was being pulled across the table and then... all quiet. I turned to my co-worker and asked, "Did they just hang up on us?" The response on the line was from the assistant, "No John. I'm still here." Mr. $#&@..#@ er! (My new name for him) decided he would not speak to anyone at a level lower than Deputy Director of a State Agency! WHAT?

So, without any direction, after traveling to the Chicago area to meet with members of a large union's negotiating team and expecting to settle a contract, I had to go to the other side, apologize and schedule additional meetings only after I could make sense of where my "leader" wanted to go.

Unbelievable but true. There were many other stories with this guy. Screaming sessions with the team were the norm. Team members often acted out of pure fear.

A few weeks later, his assistant called me wanting a conference call regarding another union. I told him (only half-jokingly) that it wouldn't work since I made it a rule to never talk with someone OVER the level of Deputy Director! There was dead silence and then (luckily for me!) the assistant chuckled (ever so slightly)! When I did make that call, Mr. (see derogatory name above) berated one of our team members so badly she broke out in tears. Our negotiating session went nowhere that day as well.

So why tell the tale of this guy? In my view, he was the worst example of a team leader. The fact he held a high-ranking position in State government notwithstanding, he was not a person to imitate. He made no attempt to lead his team by consensus, only by fear. He was a bully. And where is he now? Out of any position dealing with the human race, I hope. Other than that, I don't know and don't care.

To me, a leader of a negotiating team must be, in no particular ranked order: a friend, a listener, a reassuring voice, a leader, while also inspiring trust - Trust that you will represent everyone on the team. Just as you need to have confidence in your team - your team needs to feel that same confidence in you.

This was the standard I tried to reach. With this guy setting such a low bar, it was easy to aim higher!

Has to be a Rule in here somewhere! There is.

Rule #6 Know your team!

7ᵀᴴ RULE FOR REACHING RESOLUTIONS

How good is your word?

I mean, everyone takes a stand at some point, but then something comes up. Whatever it is, it changes everything, right?

We *are* as good as our word. Until something changes.

Then it's not our fault. We're only responsible for what we can control, if something beyond our reach alters our circumstances, well then IT'S NOT OUR FAULT.

I know a lot of people. You know a lot of people. Together we both know a lot of people. Do you know anyone who lies? I do and I bet you do, too. But if you asked every one of them if they lie, *all* of them would deny it. Am I right? No one ever admits to being dishonest. Don't believe me? Just ask them!

It's kind of funny, or real sad. But, it seems there's always a reason to justify our shifting positions. I think most of us mean well, that is, most of the time we have the best of intentions but sometimes things happen. And so we change our positions.

After all, nothing is certain, nothing lasts. "It's OK," we say to ourselves or anyone listening.

We just couldn't help it. I understand. I'm certainly not judging. I've done it too. But if we really want to reach a resolution, well, we have to be true to our word. I know it's sometimes hard to do. Doing the right thing often is.

Take a look at President Obama. I'm sure he meant every word during his campaign and many speeches after his election, talking about his vision for the Affordable Health Care Act. I believe he was sincere. He certainly sounded sincere. He wanted everyone to like his plan, so he reassured us repeatedly. Remember his sound bites "You can keep your Plan?"

And, (equal opportunity critique on the opposite party) remember the first Bush President - the "Read my lips: NO new taxes" comment?

When you take a stand, you need to be true to your word. Because, it's now *on* you. No one wants to hear the excuses, the government's red tape, website misfire, or some faceless bureaucracy. Once you start backsliding, it's over. Whatever trust you had built up, it falls away. And it's hard to restore.

Don't believe me? Talk to those people whose medical insurance plans were cancelled, talk to those who were recently told they couldn't keep their doctors or their medical plans.

Who will they believe now? If you say it, you own it. That's it, done. You can't backslide away and expect the other side to go along. Whenever we negotiate a multimillion labor agreement at the bargaining table or negotiating your way to reaching your own resolutions in your own personal life, the most important asset we bring to the table is our Word.

It's that important and it's that simple.

This Rule should be obvious:

Rule #7 Keep Your Word

8ᵀᴴ RULE FOR REACHING RESOLUTIONS

It's Day #1 and I'm meeting with a union and responding to their initial set of proposals. I begin to tell them that we are unable to agree to their proposals, one after another. Before I can finish my response to their, once again, *initial* set of proposals, the other side's negotiator starts yelling and says, "If you aren't going to agree to any of our proposals, then we should just go to arbitration!"

Arbitration! We're still discussing our initial sets of proposals AND they want to go to arbitration! You know the process, where the two parties to a negotiation hire a third party to arbitrate or decide who's right and who's not.

What do we do now?

Remember Rule #1 Don't Take It Personally? I remembered and so I didn't. I told my counterpart - "I listened to your proposals and your response to ours, now you get to listen to me." And then I finished my response.

Later that day, my team wanted to know why he had acted this way. I really didn't know. Maybe his team had expectations that we would want to agree to their "reasonable" proposals.

Maybe he was just letting our side know he was a tough negotiator and was not going to be pushed around.

But he hadn't agreed to ANY of our proposals.

So I told my team: No one agrees to the other side's initial proposals. Certainly not on Day 1!

Why is that? Well, I always ask for more than I can reasonably expect to get. And you can count on the other side doing the same thing!

Why would I ask for more than I think I'll get? So I can trade away the proposals I don't need for the one's I want. And also to trade away those proposals I don't need for getting the other side to trade away the proposals I don't want to accept. Again, trust me; they're doing the same to you.

Sound confusing? It's really not. It's almost a kind of game.

So back to our question, what do we do now?

Both sides have to agree that we have reached an impasse before proceeding to arbitration. As long as I continued to respond to their proposals, maybe even offering counter proposals and showing some progress, we'll continue to meet.

There may be some items they proposed that we can counter. And I'll press them to also begin to agree to some of ours as well. The key is learning what the other side REALLY wants!

If you simply ask them, they'll tell you: "We Want It All!" Unless we plan on giving them everything they want, we need to narrow their list down.

I start the process by proposing a "package" proposal. Maybe I'll say, "I'll agree with your proposal #4 if you agree with our proposal #7 AND you withdraw your proposals #2 and #9. Or something like that.

While the other side won't always agree to the package, their response will begin to give me an idea where there may be some movement on their part or indicate what proposal of theirs is important or conversely not so important.

It's this trial by error process that will get the process moving and allow you to discover what they really want. Remember, they may say they want it all, but this back and forth will identify what's really important to them.

This brings us to our next Rule:

Rule # 8 What Do They Want?

9ᵀᴴ RULE FOR REACHING RESOLUTIONS

We've dealt with getting the other side to say yes.

What about when you have to say NO? Saying NO to the other side is easy.

But how do you tell your own side No? You're their representative. The one who's supposed to get them what they want. And now you want to tell them No?

Can't be done? Or can it?

When I negotiate, I do listen to what my side wants. I include every one of their proposals. In fact, it's not uncommon for my side to have more proposals than the other side.

A coworker once asked me why I submitted all those proposals when I knew we wouldn't be able to get agreement on all of them. I do it because that's what my team wanted. It's important that they know I'm on their side.

And when I include their proposals I also ask them a key question. What are you willing to give up in order to get what you want? It's important that my side begins to think in those terms.

Of course, every team member usually says "We HAVE to have it and we don't want to give up ANYTHING." "OK", I say. But I ask the question anyway.

During the back and forth of negotiations, my side will see that I'm pursuing their proposals and they are also hearing what the other side says in response to their proposals.

If what they're proposing has merit - in the other side's view - we may in fact get it. If the other side doesn't see it, then we probably won't.

At some point, we may be able to get something but we need to also think about what can we live without? Thinking in those terms helps my side in determining whether what they thought they wanted is actually worth the price to get it.

And if my side wants to continue the fight, I continue the fight. But if we are getting close to an overall resolution and it becomes apparent to me that we won't get what my team member wants, I have to tell them "No" we just aren't able to get what they wanted.

It's never easy to say "No" but if I've carried their proposal to the table; fought during every session to get what they want; saying "No" is a little easier.

And, it is easier for my team member to accept because I've represented them well.

You might be thinking, "That's all well and good. But, what about when someone on the team comes up with a totally ridiculous proposal, something that is so out there you can't possibly bring it to the table without setting the negotiation process back centuries?"

Maybe that's a bit extreme. But it has happened. Here's the Rule:

Rule # 9 Just Say No!

PART 4

REACHING YOUR RESOLUTION!

10TH RULE FOR REACHING RESOLUTIONS

Stay Away From CA! Closure Anxiety, that is. And it's very real. It happens a lot. And I don't think it happens only to those who negotiate contracts.

What is it exactly? It's the inability to close the deal. One or both sides freeze up. Really freeze up, no movement. No one wants to settle... anything.

CA is serious. There should be a telethon raising funds and awareness. But until that happens, it's up to this book to make you aware. How does this happen?

It happens in so many ways.

- Maybe I'm not sure about ending the negotiations just yet.
- Or maybe I've forgotten something,
- Or more likely, I'm not sure IF I forgot something so I'll slow the process down.
- Or I'm afraid I'm not getting the best deal possible.
- Or I'm worried my team won't be happy with the final result.
  - Or I need to re-check with my principals and get their final OK.
  - OR I just can't pull the trigger!!!!

Bottom line, I've got CA and I'm a wreck!

I once negotiated with a particular union representative over a number of contracts. There were at least twenty of contracts over the years. And towards the end, the routine was always the same. After identifying his goals or needs and answering them, I would ready the teams (mine and his) for final resolution. And every time he would start to get anxious. He would throw out new proposals or new demands. Or new objections to problems we had already addressed.

He was a very experienced negotiator, until the end. Then, he was the poster child for CA. Why would he do this?

Well, it really didn't matter why, what was important is that I needed to recognize it and address his new concerns.

Now this doesn't always mean I had to give up something to him. But it did mean I had to reassure him he was getting a good deal, that I had addressed his stated concerns. Coax him to the finish line.

And it's happened to me as well. I once suffered from it big time during one contract negotiation after I made a huge mistake during a previous contract negotiation. I was too afraid to move forward and finish. And that wasn't the only time.

So, is closure anxiety really just being super cautious? No, CA prevents the sides from finishing. It's like being stuck on a ledge, unable to come down. You're afraid to move – you don't want to jump and don't know how to get back inside. You have to be coaxed back to safety. The best way I've been able to avoid this is to be prepared.

Always be prepared: Prepared to begin negotiations; Prepared for each day of the negotiations and finally; Prepared to finish the negotiations.

And that brings us to this final Rule. I told you there were 10.

Rule #10 is this: Stay Away from CA!

I STILL CAN'T GET THEM TO AGREE WITH ME!

OK, now you've got the 10 Rules. But, are you still wondering how to get the other side to agree with you?

Remember Rule #8 is: **Know what the other side wants.**

OK, you've done that. You know what they want.

Now, how do you get them to agree to what you want? Will they ever say yes?

Ever hear of the strategy "win/win?" I use to say that a lot. Perhaps not in the way it was originally meant. Let me give you an example. It's just a hypothetical example. It's not about anyone I worked with. I don't want any negative letters.

Let's say *hypothetically* you have a coworker who once *hypothetically* mentioned he/she wanted to go out after work with the rest of your group but was never asked. And the truth was, no one really wanted to ask him/her to go out with the group. So you asked him/her to come out with the group but he/she declines! Apparently she only wanted to be asked! For whatever reason!

It's a win/win! He/She wins because they were asked; your group wins because he/she's not coming!

I know, this probably isn't what the person who first coined the term meant but it is a win/win.

For our purposes of reaching resolutions, an ideal win/win is a scenario where both sides come away feeling like they achieved some or part of what they originally wanted.

Now back to our question, will they ever say yes? They will if you give them something they want. Not everything, but something.

What can we give them? I start by giving them something that is of the least importance to us. I give up something we can live without and that won't cause too much turmoil to our side.

And then I work up from there.

My goal is to give up what I don't care about and try to get what I do care about. I imagine this is what horse trading must have been like.

Of course the other side is doing the same thing, so eventually if we're successful, we'll meet somewhere in the middle.

And that's really all there is to it. Sounds easy enough, doesn't it?

It's back and forth - trying to figure out what your side can give up vs. what the other side wants that can be difficult.

So we won't get everything we want? That's correct.

And, believe me; you should never go into negotiations expecting to get everything.

Now I *have* had team members who said, "We want everything our way. We want our proposals accepted because it's what we want and we know better and we want to reject everything the other side wants because they won't work for us.

Sometimes, those who are new to the negotiating process believe that if a proposal is logical and makes sense (to them) then the other side will be compelled to agree to our logical explanation. Maybe it works in theory but it's not how it works at all in real life.

In the end those folks either come on board or they're left behind.

To reach a resolution, both sides have to come out of the process believing they came away with something of some value.

Reaching resolutions is the result of simply determining if what you want is worth giving up something. Determining if what you want is worth the price!

I once sat across the table from a union that was negotiating their first contract with my employer. They expected I would agree to all of their demands because those demands were taken from a different union contract which my employer had previously agreed. A contract that had over 30 year's maturity or seasoning, if you will. That's just a high sounding term that means the contract had been negotiated, and was in existence, for over 30 years.

Their rationale was since we had already agreed to these proposals with the other union so we were "obligated" to give them the same terms!

They had expected that I would agree to all of it by day 2 of our sessions, even while we were still discussing initial proposals! They were not being very realistic. Did I give in? No! Were they upset? ANGRY with me was more accurate. They even called my supervisor to complain about me. They said something about not negotiating in good faith.

I had tried nicely to tell them that there was no way I was going to agree to items in their first contract that the other union had to wait decades to get. They just weren't going to get the same terms without going through the process. Nothing was automatic!

Why would I take a hard stance with them? After all, we had already agreed to these very same proposals in other contracts.

To be honest, as this was their first contract, I had to dampen their expectations a bit. I had to make them work to get these proposals! Because there were items I needed to get for my side and I needed the union to feel that giving me what I needed was worth what they were going to get back!

I've had members of the team flat out say "We are not going to give that up!" "Never, Never, Never!!"

As already mentioned, to reach any resolution, if we are truly expecting to get what we want, we also need to be prepared to give something up in return. I've found this to be true both in negotiations and in life.

If we choose to not give something up, well then maybe what we thought we wanted wasn't that valuable to us after all. The choice is ours to make.

So what are you prepared to give up?

YOU DID WHAT??

You Did What?? This was so incredible I have to repeat the question.

Remember the chapter about saying NO to your team. Saying No is never easy but sometimes you have to say it. With proper preparation, it can be manageable.

What do you do when a team member wants something that's so out there, you can't believe it? You're just stunned?

Here's what happened to me.

I'm negotiating a new contract with another labor union. The group of employees in this unit had just filed to organize as a separate bargaining unit or group of employees covered by this contract. So the union's list of proposals pretty much asked for things we had already agreed to in other contracts. Not uncommon.

One of their proposals they wanted was Shift Differential pay. In other words, we would pay a higher rate if the employee worked the 3rd or late night shift. Typical shifts in our 24 hour institutions were 7a to 3p; 3p to 11 p and; lastly 11p to 7 a. So Shift Diff pay for the 3rd shift was not uncommon. This type of pay was usually given at Institutional (Correctional and Mental Health) facilities.

So, my team discusses this and we decide we would not agree to Shift Diff pay at this particular stage of the negotiations.

Then, one of our members speaks up and says, "I would rather give them Shift Diff pay when they work the regular (day) shift because that's when most of the work gets done and not at night when the residents are sleeping."

Thinking this member was joking, I laughed. We all laughed. And I said that would never happen. Ever. We would never agree to it.

This should be end of this story. It isn't. Turns out she wasn't joking.

That team member went and committed the greatest negotiations violation possible by going to the union and suggested they ask for DAY Shift Diff pay and the employer (us) would agree to it!

I've *never* had one of my team members go behind my back and have conversations with the other side without my knowledge. Not to mention, ignoring my rules given at the beginning of negotiations - including the one about there being only ONE negotiator, ME. (The employee was new to labor relations but should have known better.)

I didn't find out about this until after the contract was settled. The union told me. They were shocked that a member of my team would go to them and ask them to make such a proposal.

And quickly getting over their "shock," at the next session, the union then asked for shift diff pay for working the Day shift - even though they later told me the proposal didn't make sense to them either at the time.

The result was they were given a bit of leverage over us by my team member. The union now knew our team was not united.

In the end, the contract was settled. The union got some things they wanted and we got much of what we wanted.

They did not get shift differential pay for working the DAY shift. I had to pull some strings, and then my boss had to pull some strings and only then did the union finally backed off.

But, in exchange, they did get shift differential pay. "Normal" shift differential pay.

Which is exactly what they had wanted all along. We were forced to change our original position and give it to them.

I can only imagine the uproar I would have created for my employer IF I had agreed to paying a premium rate (shift differential pay) for someone working the day shift and conversely paying less to employees working the "graveyard" shift. It would have been my last contract I ever negotiated for that employer.

There is a Moral to this story:

I didn't take my team member seriously. I had never, (NOR HAD ANY ONE ELSE) ever heard of the concept of paying someone more to work the regular day shift. I had assumed this person knew that too.

However, my team member thought it a great idea and shared it with the union behind our backs.

Why would she ever have done this?

As I had said, she was new to her job. She probably wanted to prove she belonged and could make things happen.

Maybe she was trying to be nice - to the union, to all the employees on the day shift, maybe (in her mind) even to us as we tried to settle the contract.

To this day, I still don't know why she did it. But, ultimately, as the negotiator, the blame falls on me.

In hindsight, I should have been more emphatic in my NO to her. And, I should have better explained the reasons to her.

And, maybe, if she still didn't listen and I knew at that time what she did, I would have kicked her off the team.

Oh, well.

They say all's well that ends well, but really just like that old song lyric: *"She didn't have to be so nice; we would have liked her anyway..."*

MY MISTAKE

Mistakes happen. Ever hear that?

That's usually what I say when I make one. Trying to minimize the fallout, I make the appeal that everyone makes them. (I'm reminding myself now that I need to be just as understanding when someone else makes a mistake that affects me.)

Mistakes do happen.

And, yes I have made mistakes. With all of the contracts I've negotiated, all the years of experience... Oh yes, I've made mistakes. Many, many, mistakes

Once, about to settle a contract, I had written down what the final economic settlement proposal would be as directed by my superiors. I even reviewed the proposal - our final bottom line proposal - with the union negotiator. He told me he would agree to it but wanted to run it by his team before I made the official presentation at the table. OK, I said. That was normal and I understood.

Here's what happened.

At the negotiating table, reading from my notes outlining the cost of living pay increases over the 4 year term of the contract to his union team, I made a mistake. It was the first of several mistakes to be exact.

Mistake #1!

I inadvertently switched 2 dates. I said the union would get a 2% increase in January of the year instead of July of that same year! And I didn't catch my slip up. Fortunately, my colleague leaned over and began to whisper in my ear trying to tell me I had mixed the months up.

Mistake #2!

Unfortunately, I waved him off because the union rep was beginning to respond to my proposal and I wanted to get their response down in writing. After the union told me they would accept my offer, we shook hands and finished the session, I asked my colleague what he want to tell me. He told me; again, that I had mixed up the months of the increases.

Mistake #3!

Well, I looked at my notes - they were correct. So I reminded him that he was with me when I previously presented the figures to the union's negotiator and he had agreed. And I reminded him that the settlement would be the same for ALL the unions that year.

And then, still feeling pretty confident with my negotiating skills and apparently on quite the roll, I went for the grand slam and made....

Mistake #4!

I completely dropped the matter!

I dropped it, until that is; I got a call from my boss. Isn't it funny how supervisors can get your immediate attention? She told me that this union would not agree with our economic terms. What?

Yes, this union was holding out and demanding that we give them the pay increase in January of the year and not July like every other union!! Incredible!

I called the union rep and asked what was going on. He said that his team wrote down what I had said and his bargaining unit voted and approved the settlement with my mistake in it! But, I protested, "I had told you prior to the session and you agreed"! "Yes," he said, "until you gave us better terms!"

And he wasn't willing to back down. Too late he said, maybe if I had come to him sooner...

We had to pay his unit the same increase of 2% that every other union received that year but 6 months earlier! It was a real coup in his mind. And it was my entire mistake, it was all on me.

1. If only I had read my own writing correctly!
2. If only I had stopped to listen to my colleague!
3. If only I wasn't in a hurry to finish this contract!
4. If only I took the time to follow up with the union and ask them what they had heard at the table!
5. If only I corrected my mistake and let them know at the time that we were only agreeing to what was in my original proposal!
6. If only I didn't make mistakes!

Do I think the union took advantage of me? Absolutely! But it was my mistakes that led to my employer paying more for this contract. I didn't follow up.

And my colleague, what's he up to? When I left that agency, he was my boss!

Pretty sure he learned from my mistake. Mistakes do happen, it's what you do to correct them that counts.

My mistake!

HOW TO DEAL WITH MISERABLE PEOPLE

This chapter is NOT about those people who create some difficulty in our lives. You know, those people that are annoying but not real bad. The "know it alls": Highly opinionated, never wrong, etc. No, not even them.

Maybe the chapter should have been titled "How to handle "A" holes!" You know, the type of person that James Altucher (www.jamesaltucher.com) calls a "crappy person." (A great definition by the way!) I first read about "crappy" people in Altucher's book "Choose Yourself". It's someone you wouldn't want to spend 5 minutes with. A real A-hole!

I've known a few people like that. I'm sure you do too. You know, those people that make everyone else extremely miserable. Really, what's their deal?

Here's one that I know.

This guy was married, had kids, lived his life doing nothing but criticizing, bullying and complaining. Always the victim, he used that to play on people's sympathies. And it worked, until they got tired of his constant carping and refusal to do anything to improve his lot in life. But he couldn't always be the victim, if he got better.

Why's he like that? Not sure, I mean, he complains about everything and everyone so it's hard to narrow down the root cause. Maybe he had an unhappy childhood, maybe he's paranoid. It really doesn't matter.

End result: No longer married, kids don't speak to him. Unwilling to take any responsibility for his actions, he's now all alone.

He's ended up in his current situation entirely because of individual choices he's made throughout his life.

By the way, this is true for all us. We are "Here" because of *Our* choices.

I have helped him along the way. So have others. But, eventually, everyone just gets worn down by the constant backstabbing, lying, carping.

Altucher says most of the difficult/crappy people in our lives are the people we are close to. Think about it. Who gives you the most agita? The most grief? Your boss, neighbor, family member? The people who upset us the most are the ones closest to us. You can be mad at politicians, the Korean dictator or whomever. But they don't keep us up at night worrying because we're not particularly close to them.

So what to do?

According to Altucher, the choice is simple, the doing can be difficult. There are 2 ways to deal with people like that.

1. Don't react to them.
2. Avoid them.

So back to my guy, I tried to not react, Number 1 above, right? I tried. I really did, but it was just too hard for me to do.

I wanted to respond to everything he said to me and I sometimes did. When I reacted, I got upset. Playing over and over in my mind what he did, what I said, what I'll say the next time.

Here's my deal.

If I'm upset, I don't sleep well because I'm thinking about whatever or whoever is upsetting me. When I don't sleep well then the next day goes south. If the day goes south then I'm tired, if I'm tired... well you get it. Enough of these kind of days and I become the *That Miserable Person* that even I don't want to deal with.

I had to learn to control my reactions. That was my struggle. I finally got to the point where I simply realized it was useless for me to continue hitting my head against the wall.

So I turned to the 2nd option: I minimized contact. That proved far easier for me. Either learn how to deal with them or...leave them alone. Minimize your contact with them.

But I can't leave my.... (Job, friends, sibling, etc.) OK. I completely understand. Then you need to change your reaction whenever you're with them. It's how you react to them that ends up causing all the grief.

Think of it this way: If you don't react to their crappy - ness, are you still angry? No, because you now have taken control of your reaction.

And yes, it is hard to do! It is, and even though I'm writing this, I struggle with it daily. My only recourse sometimes is to minimize contact. That's what works for me.

I wrote on my blog about my resolutions for the New Year and how I wanted to be happy and avoid the "crappy" people. I received a reader response stating being happy must be easy for me as I must have the "means" to be happy and that not everyone is able to be happy. I interpreted that she meant that with all that goes on in our world, life is hard. And the people may be crappy because of things beyond their control. That is a valid point.

I appreciated the feedback; I truly think we all have the ability to be happy. It isn't about the means - money, fame, or success. Can we be happy watching a sunset? Or by being grateful for what we do have? Watching our children grow?

And the circumstances we find ourselves in, whether from birth or later in life, it simply is not an excuse to be unhappy.

Life is already hard so why not choose to be happy? For me, I'd rather be happy than angry or upset.

Bottom-line, I don't want to deal with difficult or miserable people. I will try to control my reaction, maybe attempt to improve the situation but if it doesn't work and I'm starting to get angry, then I minimize contact. Am I "running away?" Maybe, but remember my goal is to be happy. Not win every fight.

Again, if someone is so miserable and decides they must make everyone else's life miserable then why would anyone want to deal with them? Why would you? I don't anymore.

Having said that, I do acknowledge: In my circle of family and friends - I do have to be on my guard that I'm Not the Miserable/Crappy/A'hole Person! And the best way to do that is to work on being happy.

So back to that guy I know. After I minimized contact the results came in: I'm sleeping better, I feel better and he, well ...he's the same.

I'M MAD AS HELL!
(AND I'M NOT GOING TO TAKE IT ANYMORE!)

Whenever I think about the "old days" my memory is of no one being angry. I remember my grandmother laughing heartily before reaching up and grabbing my face with both hands saying "Oh my, what chubby cheeks! I just love to squeeze them!" (I didn't think they were that chubby) Then she let me have the spearmint candy in the dish on the end table. Everyone was happy and jolly. Always! My face was always rosy and red!

However, today is totally different. It's competitive, more stressful, and more combative. Everyone seems so angry about everything.

I've been at the negotiating table when I've gotten upset with the other side. I mean to say Angry! Angry Mad! I don't even remember what set me off - I think they had proposed something which would have set civilization back hundreds of years or something like that. I had forgotten that it was only a proposal!

I was angry/mad that they PROPOSED it! For all I know now, the union most likely did what I regularly did - propose something extreme just to get their minds off what I really wanted.

I once did this to a nice guy. And yes, even unions have nice guys.

Anyway, we were negotiating a contract and our side had just lost an important arbitration grievance case - so naturally I proposed language that would completely reverse what his side won in the arbitration. By going after his big prize, this arbitration win, I figured I could get something else in return when I ultimately backed off. I could maybe use that proposal as leverage. I warned my team what I was going to do and to take notes on his reaction.

And what a reaction it was! I had never seen a human face turn as many colors as his did that day! He began reading the proposal; his face went from white to red to purple with blue mixed in. He started stuttering and then yelled "NO! NO! NO!" And with that he ripped up my proposal! In A Thousand Pieces!

Wow, I wasn't prepared for that! I asked him if ripping my proposal meant he was refusing to negotiate. In good faith? It took him a few moments but he began to realize what his anger had done. By ripping my proposal, refusing to accept it, he had put himself in a box. It would be easy for me to argue that by doing what he did, he WAS refusing to negotiate in good faith. And so, I did just that. That day I filed an Unfair Labor Practice (ULP) charge against him with the State's Labor Board. The Board which oversees all public sector labor relations activity.

This poor guy, now he had the ULP charge to deal with as well as asking me for another copy of the proposal! His team was not happy with him and I'm sure they were furious with me.

Bottom line - I made the proposal to get him upset, I just didn't think he would get that ANGRY. When we finished the contract, I ultimately agreed to withdraw the ULP charge with some other concessions and he agreed to language which effectively reversed his big arbitration win.

WIN/WIN? For me, Yes. We got the language change we wanted and I learned a big lesson on anger.

The lesson? Whenever I allow my anger to get the best of me, I lose. Every time. No...Matter...What.

But anger can be good too, right? Well, yes, anger harnessed can be a useful tool in negotiations. Anger is an emotion. Emotions aren't good or bad. They're part of being human. As long as we are in control of our emotions, our anger, we're good. If we lose control though, we're probably taking things personally too.

Don't get mad.

BE CAREFUL WHAT YOU ASK FOR!
(OR ANOTHER MISTAKE MADE)

I negotiated a contract for another agency some years ago. I was anxious to let everyone know - the agency, my employer and especially, my boss - that I was good. Real good.

So I went all out. I gave the union a set of proposals that would effectively take away items we gave them in the last contract. It's all about the winning, I thought. Right?

Now in all honesty, giving proposals that are hard hitting is not uncommon. I do it all the time. The difference here was the why.

I wasn't trying to use my hard proposals as leverage to back the other side off, to get them to withdraw their own proposals. No, I wanted to take away things. Things we had already given them in previous contracts.

I envisioned my boss slapping me on the back, welcoming me into the good old boys and girls club of great negotiators.

Here's what I did. In the previous contract, we gave the employees an incentive. If they did not use any of the 12 sick days they earned in a calendar year, we would give them one day off to be used as a personal day in the next calendar year. It was an incentive day encouraging them to not use any sick time in a year.

So I proposed we would remove the extra day off. Why?

Well, as I explained to the union, the state was in a financial crisis. We needed to cut costs and here was one way we could do that.

The State of Illinois had approximately 40,000 employees who received this incentive benefit. The agency I was representing had all of 130 employees. This financial "savings" was not going to add up to anything substantive. Yet I insisted.

This is what happened…

On the first day of negotiations, after I explained why I proposed rescinding this incentive day off - the union agreed! They signed off on it the very first day! So I accepted. I knew my boss would be pleased that I "took" something away. No other union in Illinois had this benefit taken away!

Not only that, I was so ecstatic for having taken something away, I began to bully and intimidate the union's negotiator. One minute I'd joke with him and the next I would get angry with him. I was putting on a show.

Turns out their guy was negotiating his first contract. He was nervous, somewhat unsure of himself and I took advantage. I tried to embarrass him. It was all about winning. And winning meant taking things away.

That's what I thought; at least I did until I talked to my boss. He was not pleased at all.

He asked me, "Why in the world would you do that?" I fumbled for an answer but only came up with something about taking something from them! And I had given up nothing to get it!

So he began to educate me in the world of labor relations - "Why would we want an agency of 130 employees to not have a benefit that 39,870 other employees already have? This administration (read: Governor) wanted every employee to have the same benefits!

He went on to lecture me that, "It's not smart negotiating if I don't negotiate with the big picture - the entire state in mind." I needed to know the direction my principals wanted to go and fit my negotiations into the overall plan. And he said more sternly, "We never try to embarrass the other side. After these negotiations are done, we still have to work together."

So what I thought was a real coup - taking something away - really wasn't. I didn't stop to analyze what direction my superiors were going. And fit my negotiations into that direction.

I overreached trying to impress. I ended up not impressing anyone.

I wanted to fight to get noticed. I got noticed but not for the right reason.

I was trying to WIN and *not* trying to reach a resolution. I had to learn I didn't have to argue or fight to get ahead.

MIXED MESSAGES

I know what you're thinking. Mixed messages, you get them all the time. Everyone gets them. One time or another.

And, if you're trying to reach a resolution you're going to get them too.

I've spoken to a number people working for a living who believe their upper management just doesn't seem to know what they're doing. What? How could the bosses not know?

"Why are we changing directions?" "We can't possibly do more work without hiring more headcount." Or this, "We hired more headcount but now we have to spend time training the new employees and we can't possibly get our goals accomplished. Why doesn't management understand? Doesn't anyone know what they're doing?"

So back to reaching resolutions, are you getting similar mixed messages?

When I'm working to reach a contract resolution I listen to my principals. Always. I even tell the other side; I have to check with my principals, or in other words the "boss." They are the ones who are giving me direction.

Whenever I negotiate I attempt to gain an advantage for my side. Or I try to stop the other side from gaining an advantage.

But what if I don't understand their direction? Or what if it seems yesterday's direction is now changed today. Are they lying? Or don't they know what they're doing? Yes, you may be told one thing one day, another thing tomorrow. This especially happens when the principals are new. It's because as they experience the learning curve their positions and their directions change. But if I don't understand their directions, I cannot reach a satisfactory resolution.

And it may not just be with the principals. Sometimes it's with co-workers, the ones who are always trying to get ahead. Sometimes they do by kissing up. "I'll do that!" Or "let me do this too!"

They are so intent on getting ahead; they forget you're there too. They may be they're afraid of making a mistake or simply wanting to be noticed. And so they're giving mixed messages too.

After a pause and a deep breath or three, I realize they are just like me. They're making decisions based on what they know; what direction they're being given and also just like me, they basing their decisions on their own fears and expectations.

So back to mixed messages, sometimes I get conflicting directives. It can be very frustrating. And the key to dealing with it is to not get upset but try to gain a perspective on the reasons for the mixed messages.

It took me awhile but I began to understand the nature of mixed messages. Now whenever I get them, I try to remember the only 2 possible reasons for them. And you will definitely thank me when you read how simple this really is.

In my career I've discovered there are, in fact, only 2 possible explanations and they apply to each and every situation involving mixed messages.

Maybe my principals did know more than me. Maybe they had access to the bigger picture and knew of how my area fit in within the company's overall larger goal. Maybe my concerns were dwarfed in the overall scheme. So the first one is:

1. Your principals are way smarter than you. Way Smarter.

They know more about the bigger picture than you do. They actually do have all the answers.

OR

2. They don't know sh*t about anything. They really do not know anything at all about what they are directing you to do.

It's that simple.

Your course of action is exactly the same with both.

They are your boss. You follow their directives. Today. Tomorrow. And for as long as you are working for them.

In either instance, my responsibility is to gently let them know my concerns, the risks and anticipated outcomes.

And then let them direct me. If I was proven wrong, well it means my principal was right. See number 1 above.

If it turns out I was right, see number 2 and know that you did offer your advice. Either way you'll be covered.

Reaching resolutions shouldn't be hard. It truly doesn't have to be. It becomes hard when we fight back. Or get angry because we don't understand the big picture.

My advice is to relax and know mixed messages happen all the time.

If you still find it hard to deal with them after reading this then you need to reread Rule #1 and Rule #2 of this book and just don't take it personally.

MAKING THIS FIT

Let's look at the 10 Rules once again.

1. Don't take it Personally!
2. DON"T TAKE IT PERSONALLY! I Really Mean It!
3. Know The Language
4. Know What's Real
5. Know What you Want
6. Know Your Team
7. Keep Your Word
8. What Do They Want?
9. Just Say No!
10. Stay Away From CA!

These Rules are meant to simplify the process of reaching your resolutions. Even if you're not going to negotiate a contract but want to find your way in life remember this: *We're all looking for resolutions.*

These Rules can help you stay on point to reach those resolutions, to be successful.

Sure you'd say, but these rules won't all apply. I don't have a team! OK, maybe you don't have one. But does the other side have a team? Whoever you are using to help you is in fact a member of your team. I'll grant that these 10 Rules may not *all* apply to your *every* given situation. I'd wager though that most of them will.

A point I've attempted to make in this book is that you don't have to be a professional negotiator to get to your resolution.

After all, I did it. I wasn't intending to have a career in labor relations – negotiating contracts, hearing and resolving employee grievances. I fell into it. Turns out after several years I might have developed a knack for it. But it was because I recognized these Rules that I was able to have any success in it.

All I ask is you give them a try and see if they won't work for you too. Helping you to *reach your resolution*.

FROM ME TO YOU

I wrote this book to share what I've learned about reaching resolutions. What worked, what didn't, my mistakes and thoughts.

I have to admit I found it very difficult putting myself "out there." It's kind of scary creating something and holding it out to others. It was almost like running for political office, you're successful if a little over 50% support you – which means close to half didn't. I did it anyway because I think I have something to share, something useful. I do hope you agree.

I only ask that you try out these rules, to see if they work also for you. As I've said, I believe they will.

And if you do, I'd wager you'll soon emerge with that incredible feeling of satisfaction when you reach that resolution you'd been seeking.

If you'd like to contact me, you can do so at:
   Twitter: @reachingresblog

My Blog: www.reachingresolutionsblog.com
   Sign up and receive the posts by email.

Email at: reachingresolutionsblog@gmail.com

Face Book: Reaching Resolutions Blog.com
    Please "Like" our Facebook page, too!!

And lastly, I would be very honored if you would review this book on Amazon.
    Thank you.
    JT

Notes

Notes

Notes

No one gives up anything without expecting something in return. So the question is always: Is what you want worth the price you'll have to pay?

www.ingramcontent.com/pod-product-compliance
Lightning Source LLC
Chambersburg PA
CBHW051731170526
45167CB00002B/895